Modern Publishing
A Division of Unisystems, Inc.
New York, New York 10022
Series UPC: 19615

The big top's up, the lights are down,
The smile is set on every clown.
Tickets, please, and take your seat.
The band strikes up a happy beat!

1 ringmaster greets the crowd.
2 big lions roar out loud!

The **3** ring circus has begun,
With lots of fun for everyone!

4 silly monkeys hang around,
Way up high above
   the ground.

5 long trunks are raised up high,
And water showers from the sky.

6 clowns balance carefully. The top one smiles and waves at me!

7 seals catch seven balls.
They spin around, but not one falls!

8 white horses proudly prance.
Their plumes wave in their stately dance.

9 balloons float way up high.
9 silly clowns wave good-bye.

10 musicians play a tune.
A well-trained cow jumps over the moon!

11 dogs jump through a hoop,
And all the chickens fly the coop.

12 happy children, row on row,
Clap and cheer the circus show.

The big parade is marching by.
How many numbers can you spy?

It's time to take the big top down
And move on to another town.
Good-bye!